Happy Birthday Col

I hope you
enjoy these Midday Poet Musings

Lots of Love
Rebecca x

"These poems explore the themes that are characteristic of his poetry: nature, identity, love, loss, mythology and his love of cinema. Lewis observes the world around him, meditates in silence and translates his emotions into words and imagery. With his poetry – as with his painting – Lewis attempts to discover identity and to express his sensitivity through hidden messages, leaving us wondering which mysterious clues could open things up. In fact, Lewis writes in his poem The Poets: *"They bathe in mysteries while others only seek to explain them."* If Lewis' poems are mysterious and intriguing, they are also rich and magical. A joy to explore.

- Nathalie Banaigs – Culture in Kent

"A fascinating collection that lurches gleefully from lurid imagery to painful innocence, from complex visions to penetrating simplicity. Bill Lewis is a fucking genius."

- Dr. Aidan Hehir

"Funny, ironic and no-holds-barred, Bill Lewis' poetry (and surprise singing!) left us in awe.

- The Kent Arts Conference

"Bill Lewis' poetry has a very special lilt, flow, and intensity of feeling. Read or listen to it carefully and you hear a seraphic, Hassidic voice that whispers cries and sings HOLY HOLY HOLY in the living speech of his own time"

- Michael Horovitz

Bill Lewis' new poetry is as magical as ever, beautiful, innovative, and disturbing in turn. It's the work of a poet with the paintbrush of a surrealist, spotlights on harsh reality juxtaposed with surprising, evocative imagery. Love and war, myth, movies and Medway are given the classic touch by one of Kent's best poets.

- Maggie Harris

"Bill Lewis has the true soul of a poet (and not in a bullshitty way of some poets I could name) I love the mix of biography, personal folklore, shadow projection, symbolism, reportage ... inspirational stuff."

– Graham Joyce

"If you swim into Bill Lewis' poetic river, you'll come upon moons and trains, flags and crosses, wars and flowers, suitcases and foxes, coffee and stones. In his poems every being, every object becomes pregnant with rich new meaning. Bill Lewis writes tender, compassionate meditations that reconcile us with chaos and the unknown."

- Alicia Partnoy

"Bill Lewis's wide-ranging, truthful, plain-speaking work demonstrates the strengths of a profound connection and attachment to place."

– Peter Straub

Sparrowhawk

Paris

Photo: Ann Lewis

Sparrowhawk

& other poems
BILL LEWIS

First published by Colony Press in 2022
Typesetting by A Mato

Produced by The Choir Press

A CIP record of this book is available from the
British Library

ISBN: 978-1-9996948-1-4

Introduction by Sarah Hehir

Bill Lewis looks at life with a fresh, critical, lyrical eye; his poems challenge the reader to do the same. It's what I want from an artist. It's the difference between taking a photo and being a photographer – the interpretation is a transformation. A great artist doesn't give us a 2D representation of what we already see. They send the world back to us, reinvigorated. It's not always nicer. Sometimes a poem written by Bill feels like a twisted world; threatening and dark.

Some poems intrusively peer, like a dentist's mirror, into my soul and it's not necessarily a place I want to go. At other times Bill dips his pen in magical realism and writes with such wicked playfulness that you can imagine him leaping and cavorting down Gillingham High Street. Or Chatham. Bill is a poet you're as likely to find in a pound shop as in a lecture theatre. A trip through any of his collections (including this one) is a journey from gutter to nirvana; from baked beans to mythos and often back again.

Bill Lewis is a shapeshifter. I suspect there is some of the shaman in him and that his spirit animals are not always purely metaphorical. When I greet a streak of orange-brown fur on the way home from an open-mic night in one of the Medway towns, the creature greets me back in a very Bill-like tone. It would surprise me, but not much, to find that Bill becomes coyote and fox, magpie, and raven. He calls his wife Bear. The clues are all there.

Bill also shapeshifts as an artist. He's a writer, a poet, a painter, photographer, printer, graphic novelist, musician, singer and more recently an image manipulator. Being a fan of Bill's work means having no room left on your walls or bookshelves. Become his friend and you surrender all hope of space and order to his generous gifts: carefully chosen books and works of art designed to lead you along his favourite paths of knowledge and learning. I choose this kind of disorder any day – to trip and break my ankle on a pile of books from Bill will only give me more time to read them.

Bill sees fluidity in gender and identity: he was exploring this through his art and poetry long before the mainstream world became interested. Born and brought up in the small Kentish village of Barming, he might be forgiven for seeing life through a parochial lens. But Bill's rural upbringing brought about the opposite; his hunger for knowledge is feral and no subject is safe. His interests are vast and varied: language, anthropology, science-fiction, ancient worlds, detective TV series, trans-fashion, revolutions, inequality, Kentish animals and on and on forever. It feels like the world around Bill is alive and conscious and that it whispers to him. His poems reflect a deep generosity in sharing his truly original observations.

Just before the pandemic, I asked Bill to come and read at the final night of a drama project I'd been leading with three local primary schools. He agreed – ever generous with his time. Our play, at the Brook Theatre, was vivid and hectic and everything you would expect from a lively group of ten-year-olds allowed to craft their own story involving animated film, flashbacks, cartwheels, danger and an old trunk of poetry. When Bill took to the stage, I hoped my young performers would listen respectfully. What I forgot is that Bill isn't after respect; he's more interested in engagement and wonder. Within minutes, the children – having never met him or been introduced to his poems - were clapping along to his shaman's drum, swaying to the rhythm of his words. It was magical. Magic. Myth. Transformation. The children still talk about it.

Bill's books and paintings are shipped and delivered around the world. As an original member of two important artistic moments – the Medway Poets and The Stuckist Movement – he has made his mark in history. However, I think the true mark of the man is his life-long commitment to knowledge and creativity and his willingness to share some of the secrets of his heart and soul with the rest of us.

This collection is particularly playful with both content and form. From the 'Ode to the Necktie' in the shape of a Windsor Knot to a poem for Delia Derbyshire: creator of the theme tune for Dr Who.

> *I heard your siren song*
> *My bags are packed*
> *And I am Skaro bound*

Humour and graceful wisdom, sit side by side in the same poem. In his list of twenty-six things that poets are, Bill tells us,

Some were born under the celestial sign of Sputnik/ which can give them untidy hair.

and my favourite,

They think major thoughts in a minor key.

So, here's to the poet. Raise a glass and let us all cavort in the company of tricksters, fools, bold coyotes and shapeshifters. Cross lines with dark edges. If you want carnival, it comes with nasty sideshows. If you want religion, you can't hide from corruption and concealed desires. That mirror Bill holds, is held up to your soul. What is it you see?

Sarah Hehir is an award-winning playwright who writes for BBC TV and BBC Radio Four. Her plays have been performed in London and Edinburgh and she regularly visits Kosovo to read poetry and lead workshops.

www.sarahhehir.com

Contents

For Chris Broderick
and
Medway, The City of Poets

Apples Pickers 1940

for Marge and Arthur Earl

As they work, above them a
Spitfire takes on a Messerschmitt.

The daily dog fights of the
Autumn days of nineteen forty.

The Spit like a great broken
Bird comes down in the orchard.

The wicker baskets fall from
Their hands, apples bruising
On wet grass as they rush to help.

They pull the pilot free from
The fuselage, he is just nineteen.

At first they think him wounded
But it is just the red hydraulic fluid.

Marge is a Land Girl and
Arthur a Reservist waiting to be

Called up. This is how they met.
It was a fruit picker's morning.

Pockets of mist in the valley.
The river Medway a white snake.

Dog

Eternal child, not growing up, just getting older.
Still running in his sleep chasing shadow-rabbits

Or that elusive tail that sometimes taunts him
Out of the corner of his deep chocolate brown eye;

That sometimes wags him as he pursues the ball;
That object that he cannot throw but tirelessly wants
Thrown: almost round; saliva slick; slow punctured.

Then there is the head shaped wedge in the chicken
Pie that you left on the counter, just for a moment;
Returning to find him sitting calmly, as if not guilty.

Night Trains

Night trains whistle as they pass each other
In the river valley, a sound more melancholy

Than a loon on a lake, as I listen, lying awake
Wondering at those lives in lighted carriages.

Down there below the churchyard, on the track
Parallel with the Medway, where the willow

Weeps its emerald tears that never touch the earth,
Night trains rattle through my un-sleep.

An owl asks *who* and from the other side of the
Wood its would-be mate answers it's *you*, and a
Glow worm glows green in the hollow of your hand.

The books on my shelf whisper stories to themselves
And mice skitter scatter in the skirting board.

In my dream I am already on board one of those
Night trains bound for some station of adventure.

Poem for Simon Mills

He throws paint at symphonic skies.
Conducting silent cloud operas with

The baton of his brush or in the hush
Of a forest clearing, finding himself

Warlocked into a woodland state of
Mind, dreaming of his dryadic

Wood-wife as she poses mythago-like
In the midst of a tree-bearded afternoon.

Estragon and Vladimir
Have left the Theatre

Godot finally got there but
Estragon and Vladimir were gone.

Put another book upon the fire
I'm getting cold, I'm getting on.

Godot was always very tardy
Estragon and Vladimir: mere
Existential Laurel and Hardy.

Obvious meaning makes me mean,
I find it just gets in the way.

Estragon and Vladimir now wait
Far away while Godot's here to stay.

Abraxas

The curtain is torn.
The cornerstone missing.

The letters fly from
The page and dance back

To the crown from
Whence they first came.

The black dog barks.
The black sun shines.

Across the still sea of brass
The blackbird wings his way,

From his orange beak
He sings these words:

I have come to break all
The clocks with a hammer

And shatter every mirror
That exists in Creation.

This Ink

This white moth
That you kept
Disguised as a star

This bright star
That you pressed
Into soot black ink

This obsidian ink
That you made
Into an alphabet

This alphabet
That you can use
To make a portal

This door is a book
Full of stolen owls
And white moths

Swashbuckling for Eight-Year-Olds

I went to see all the swashbucklers. How Burt
Lancaster's teeth flashed in *The Crimson Pirate*

As he swung down from the rigging and proclaimed;
Avast! This is a pirate tale in a pirate world!
And *Zorro* made me want a cape and mask.

After watching *The Siege of the Saxons* I spend half-a-
crown on a plastic sword (it had a fake red ruby in the
pummel) but on the way home I got into a fierce fight

With The Red Knight (a post box) and the blade
snapped in half against his heavy armour.

These days when I read *The Lord of the Rings* I smile,
Remembering that day when I took on my adversary;

Unlike Isildur's sword mine could not be re-forged.
I reckon that post box was a Norman in disguise.

Remembering Nothing Happening

On the radio the Beach Boys
     sing *Barbara Ann.*
I turn the pages of a
     Fantastic Four comic book.
Lost in Jack *King* Kirby's artwork.

Before my eyes the
     heroes battle Dr Doom.

Despite being in Margate, England,
Californian style,
     honey coloured sunlight
Streams through a dormitory window.

     Nothing remarkable happened,
Yet I remember it with pin sharp clarity
      while other
More momentous occasions
     are half forgotten.

I find myself wondering if the light really was
     so different in the 1960's
Or maybe it's that my eyes were younger.

I have no recollection of what happened just
     before or just after.

This non-event is frozen and self-contained,
I visit it often, wishing I still had the comic.

A Box of Birds

Chough

for The Wildwood Trust

So good to see a chatter of choughs playing on the
Coastal breeze above our chalk grassland, scouting for

Insects and probing with their curved scarlet beaks,
Once again into Kentish topsoil. Brythonic bird, you
Once went west and spoke for the people there.

The Cornish put you on their coat of arms but little
Bekit you were our bird too. Now you have returned to

The Downs of Kent, perhaps because *we* are wiser now
And have taken back the libel laid at your nest; it seems

You were not an arsonist after all, not an incendiary
Avian and a stealer of grain. Perhaps it was a Saxon
Slight at a bird that may be Arthur in another form.

Burning haystacks was more the style of Captain Swing
Pyrrhocorax pyrrhocorax,
                    so good they named you twice.

Magpie

Good morning to you Captain
I hope you and your good lady
And your young ones are well.

Dressed so fine in your Dominican
Inquisitors' livery, except of course
Those blacks are not as black as they

First seem. In a good light, those deep
Blues and that iridescent emerald tail
Catching sunlight as it bobs to keep
Your balance on the branch.

I wonder what theology of rainbows
You understand, what meteorological
Magic is at your command?

You answer with a cacophony of croaks
That make even crows sound like robins:

Six for the devil and seven's for God
One of them is even, the other is odd,
But I won't tell which one is which
Unless you're a gypsy, a fox or a witch.

Jackdaws

For Anthony Rudolf

Nimble and quick and a bit of a lad.
No need to jump a candlestick as
Our feathers are already scorched black.

We all have the same first name
No matter what gender, and because
Of this we affirm it at every moment:
Jack! Jack-Jack! Jack! Jack-Jack! Jack!

We all have the same first name,
Except for Franz, our Czech cousin.
He's a bit of a literary type, always
Trying to get into some castle or other.

Sparrowhawk

Suddenly the birdsong ceases; the sparrows
Seem as if they've been pulled back into
The hedge by bands of invisible elastic,
All chirping and chatter stops, the wings
Of the doves and wood pigeons whirr
As they make for safety in the trees.

I look out from the kitchen window
Where the birdfeeders, full of fat balls
And seed, swing in the silent garden.

Then I see the reason, a sparrowhawk
Has dropped like a stone from his blue home
To rest upon the fence, his yellow gaze glares
Without malice at the deserted feeders but

He is not hunting; if he had been, none would
Have seen him until he struck, swooping in
Low, like a mini stealth fighter only a centimetre
Above the grass, the displaced air parting
Stalks like an invisible comb through hair,

Rippling on the surface of the water feature.
Swifter than a swift, only rising to hit his prey
At a full fifteen kilometres an hour, leaving
Nothing but a cloud of feathers in his wake.

                    Make no mistake,
He is not hunting, he's at rest, almost seeming
To enjoy the effect his presence has upon the
Denizens of the garden;
            I realise this is anthropomorphising,

It's a human fault, just as some might demonise
This pocket predator in Disneyesque categories

Of good and bad animals. He only does
What he is designed to do: feeding to fuel flight
    as seed is not enough to hold him aloft.

Albino Crow

Albino crow
          against the snow.

There it is.   No it isn't.

          Or is it?

Tropical Fish

for David Bryant

Schools of iridescent darts:

glowlight   rainbowfish

swordtail   scissortail   golden pencilfish

harlequin   tigerbarb   angelfish

red striped-american flagfish

black and white   zebrafish

bristlenose   blackneon   bleedingheart

rosybarb   sailfin-molly   cockatoo cichlid

upside-down catfish

Compass Rose

At the edge of the night there's a dog barking.
In the Cathedral Garden; the Angel of Knives

Opens her lacerating wings and holds me
In her steel embrace and the Compass Rose

On the nautical chart of my heart points forever
In your direction; I'm a pilgrim blown between

Those houses where the four winds hold court.
I think of the miles between us and empty streets,

Of the misty stars of the east and green science
Of forests and the distant blue infinity of orchards

.

I walk by Earthlight, a prince of telephone boxes.

Two Ravens

The old man waits at the level crossing
He holds a *Sainsbury*'s carrier bag.

His house is the other side of the track.
And the train passes slowly.

In his head his thoughts and memory have
Black wings and they flap around like

Great birds caught in a confined space.
His left eye is weak due to treatment for a

Torn retina. It had not brought wisdom
But a lightning storm in his eyeball worthy

Of *Ragnarök.* He used to be somebody
But now he is eclipsed by others (some of

Whom have not hung on the great ash tree)
He still prefers *Runic* to *Monkspeak*

Each morning his two ravens are released.
He worries that one day one of them might

Fly away and not come back. Which would
Be worse, to lose *thought* or *memory?*

The Poets

after Léo Ferré

1.

Their notebooks are filled with more crossing out
than words.

2.

Some were born under the celestial sign of *Sputnik*
which can give them untidy hair.

3.

Some have imaginary friends while some are
imaginary friends to others.

4.

Some are invisible while others have vibrant plumage.

5.

One of them might pick up a book that they read in their
youth and find to their surprise, pressed between
the pages: a human nose

6.

They know that truth is better than facts
but both are trumped by kindness.

7.

In their youth they had to decide between eating lunch
or buying the book they needed to read and later
fainting from hunger.

8.

None of them have been mugged by foxes
while walking home at night.

9.

They prefer literary to literal.

10.

They know that metaphors reach ninety nine percent of
all known mysteries.

11.

Crows sometimes flew out of the paperback book they
were reading as they sat on the top deck of a bus.

12.

They think major thoughts in a minor key.

13.

They understand that a poem is a device that enables
you to breathe under the surface of a dream.

14.

They are tuned into the 14 radio stations of the cross.
Even when they are old, they write with the fountain
pen of youth.

15.

They know language is born of silence and
carries within it its DNA.

16.

Zero is their lucky number.

17.

They know that every hello has a goodbye hidden in it.

18.

Their thoughts are the colour of autumn although often
their voices are green.

19.

Even the obese ones publish their work in slim volumes.

20.

Their hearts and minds are joined by a
confluence of ley lines.

21.

They can hear the past like tiny silver trumpets playing across the misty lawns of remembrance.

22.

They adore the moon, and the moon adores them because both know that reflected light is subtle and full of mystery.

23.

They bathe in mysteries while others only seek to explain them.

24.

Poems come to them and ask to be born. They give them nice clothes, shiny shoes and a haircut and send them out into the world.

25.

They know that no one owns language, and few understand it; that some words are locked doors, and each letter has a deep chasm beneath it filled with multiple meanings.

26.

When they die they go to Paris.

Squirrel

Sciuridae scurry across
The grass: *Little grey shadows*

Your *Ratatoskr*-like leaping
From branch to branch as if

A thought jumping a synapse
In the green mind of this tree.

I once watched one of your
Species in a London Park as he

Buried a nut; patting with paws
The earth over the hole; then

Looking around at a multitude of
Fallen leaves, taking one and

Placing it carefully over the
The spot (*to hide or remember?*)

Seconds after he darted away
The wind took the leaf.

Chatham Squirrel

I wish I'd had a camera with me.
I know most people have them on
Phones these days but

I am a dinosaur dragged against
My will into the 21st Century.

A cat was chasing a squirrel along
A wall which came to a dead end
          by an adjoining house,

Where the little rodent would also
          come to a dead end.

          Just as this feline predator
Was about to strike the death blow

The squirrel spun around and punched
It on the nose; the cat jumped back.

This was not supposed to happen!
It was a *Tom and Jerry* moment.

The split-second pause was all
The squirrel needed to get ahead and
It leapt to safety.

It was a *Hanna-Barbera* moment.

It would have gone viral on *YouTube.*

It was a *Kodak* moment but alas, no camera.

Ode to the Necktie

Oh perfect Windsor knot
an upside down
pyramid of silk
with that
little
dimple in the
cloth, oh necktie
honoured descendent
of the cravat, worn at
the throats of Croatian
mercenaries on their visit
to France, where they
intrigued their Parisian
hosts, who soon began to
wear *La Cravate.* Maybe
Macaronis took you west;
soon even Yankee-doodle-
dandies wore you. Then you
went on a diet, got slimmer
became so many styles; *bolo*
Slim-Jim, string & kipper
often fixed with a neat clip;
sometimes gaudy & hand
painted with an American's
idea of a Hawaiian hula
dancer; sometimes tasteful
in plain black or white or
paisley patterned. Club; old
school or in regimental stripes.

Some saw you as a symbol
of servitude but I miss you
now that the streets seem to
teem with men in baseball
caps, shorts and T-shirts &
I often wonder if our casual
dress has made us, sometimes
too casual in our thought
& deed; any sense
of occasion
lost.

Yod

I am Yod
I am the letter removed
From your name by
The Universe. Of course,
I complained that it was
Unfair to be redacted, and
Asked if it was because I
Was the smallest in the alphabet.

Poor Yod,
The Universe replied,
It was nothing personal but I
Needed to remove you so she
Would change into someone else.

Something else.

The universe, AKA *The*
Most High placed me in His/Her
Crown until I was needed next.

I bet you never missed me.

The Implicit

There's a Torah above the Torah
One is ink and one is fire.

I'm told there are seven heavens
And they are strings upon a lyre.

There's a wave beneath the wave
Things that you can't see
      on the wall of Plato's cave.

If you doubt these words look at
How subatomic particles behave.

There's a woman in the mirror
Who wants me to join her there.

She wears a dress of feathers
      and has a library in her hair.

Magic Trick

Poetry and magic are sisters,

       and to prove it,
Ladies and Gentlemen,

For my next trick I will

Fit this huge

ELEPHANT

Into this tiny poem.

       Hey presto!

Fox Carousel

On Facebook somebody wrote:
Woke up last night to an awful
Noise, looked out of the window
And saw three foxes shrieking and
Squeaking as they ran around
              a tree in the garden.

As I read the post I imagined
A strange vulpine merry-go-round
Where the horses had been
Replaced by Reynard's children,

Three dots appeared as someone
Wrote a reply: *that's the kind of*
Thing Bill Lewis would
              write a poem about.

Hedge

The Old English and German words *Hag* and *Hex*
Come from the same word as *Hedge*.

A wise woman, a witch, is literally a *Hedge Woman*,
One who lives in liminal places,

On a border between realities most of us cannot see.

She told me to look over the hedge and asked:
What can you see? I saw the dormant part of me

Surrounded by thorns that the waking world me
Hacks at daily with a sword. Entering a palace, I pass

Several sleeping personalities and find myself in
A bedroom; a bridal suite, where I kiss a mirror.

A lip shaped circle of condensation.
A misty ghost of a mouth returns the kiss.

The glass turns to water, and I fall in.
I never learnt how to swim. Beauty wakes up in me.

We Learn The Rhythm Before The Meaning

Dali's moustache, Magritte's pipe
And Van Gogh's ear walk into a bar
The bartender exclaims,
>   *That's a bit surreal!*

A horse (with a long face)
Drowning his sorrows in bourbon
Knocks back his drink and leaves
In disgust, muttering to himself
>   *At least my story was funny.*

The Reduction of Art in the 21st Century

Dali's moustache, Magritte's pipe
And Van Gogh's ear walk into a bar
The bartender says,

You just missed them, Frida Kahlo's
Eyebrows were in earlier drinking Mescal.

The Long Week

1.

The Monday of the Blind Voyeur
When I dream of dancing in
Heaven to *Tainted Love*, dressed in a
Latex dress and a Cleopatra wig.
Or I am Mata Hari, patron saint
Of amateur spies and exotic dancers.

2.

The Tuesday of the Missing Hand
That was eaten by a wolf held captive
By an almost invisible chain made
From the sound a cat makes when it hunts,
The root of a mountain and the breath of
A fish. *Dwarf stuff*, he says, scenting it.
A time of impotence and fatherhood
When some gods get demoted while
Others climb the corporate ladder.

3.

The Wednesday of the Closed City
When all the shops are empty and
Window dressers wrestle with naked
Mannequins. Only the cinemas give
Shelter. *EMPIRE. ABC. RITZ. ODEON.*
Fleapit and the *Bug-hutch* where
Feet stick to the chewing-gummed floor
As we sit on the worn red faux velvet
Seats that are pocked with cigarette burns.

I touch your subtext and you touch mine
Beneath artificial stars chocolate-covered
Raisins melt in the palms of our hands.

4.
The Thursday of the Waiting Man,
Under the blue poem of the sky,
He whistles Bizet as he waits, his heart
Full of *L'Arlésienne* sadness and the
Turning of the windmills of autumn.
But soon his wife will brighten
The front doorway; so he ignores the
Forked lightning in his cup of tea.

5.
The Salt and Vinegar Friday
Of steamed up windows and paper.
The wind plastering my trousers
Against my limbs as I struggle home,
The Sadean rain, grey as the 1950s,
Whipping my body. I once, long ago,
Asked my mother if it would be winter
Forever. She told me that it wouldn't;
But I never really believed her.

6.
The Saturday of Sleeping Late
Dreaming of the promise of
Fictional timetables. The girl who
Delivers our paper has a purple
Paisley mini dress and white legs.
She knows that I am looking
Behind my bedroom curtain,

Smiling to herself as she goes
Out of our gate, exaggerating
Her walk; the curve of her bottom
Breaks my heart. I am 13 and a bit.
Later I will spend my 2/- pocket
Money on some *Marvel* comics.
Tonight *Dr. Who* will be on
After the interminable football
Results, although they do give
The television time to warm up.

7.
The Sunday of the Orange Teacup
Holy toast and stone bells.
Barwick Green on the big
Radio; its dial is a travelogue of
Europe. You can turn it and go all
The way to Moscow via Luxembourg.
But on my little transistor (that I
Found in a cornfield, which makes
It a magical object) I listen to pirates.

8
On one of these days, I will come to you
In my true form, in my true form,
Or not at all, or not at all, or not at all.

Rupert

Rupert, sit down, your mother and I want
To talk to you. Please take your fingers out
Of your ears, it's not the birds and bees thing
Again. Look, I'll get right to the point.
When you were a little boy, on those long school
Holidays, we loved it when you went out into
The forest around Nutwood and had all those
Imaginary adventures; little men with flying cars,
Tiger Lily and her dad *The Conjuror* and all
That sort of thing. We even smiled when
You insisted you were a bear and gave
Your little chums animal names. Although
Edward was a bit upset being cast as an elephant
Just because his surname happened to be Trunk.
But now we think you might need some help.
Your line manager phoned us, she's worried
About some of the things you've been saying
At work about mischievous Elves putting a spell
On the computers, and we think perhaps
You should see someone. A *Professional*.
Also, there is an issue about those yellow
Check pants that you insist on always wearing.

Dementia

The man who taught me how to think
Can himself no longer think.

The man who loved maps
Now gets lost in his three-room apartment.

The man who liked to read
Can no longer follow the simplest plot.

All the films he once watched have been
Remade with the same actors but with
                    the best bits edited out.

He spends hours looking for something
But he does not remember what it was.

If after I visit him some well-meaning
Evangelist should try to tell me

About a kind and caring God, I might just
Beat them to death with their own bible.

The Heart Is A House Where Our Loved Ones Dwell

For Alan and Peggy Morris

The heart is a house
            where our loved ones dwell

        While we *are* they *are*.

But they also live
            in the things they taught us

        and the love and kindness they gave.

When we in turn
            pass these gifts to others
                        they live again.

She May Be Nothing Like The Sun

She may be *nothing like the sun*

But she won't fit into fourteen lines,

Nor into any rhyme scheme

That has yet to be contrived.

She's a Beatrice upon a bridge.

A brief glimpse that lasts for many years.

An empty space next to the Throne.

And when she's in exile with her people

In that *oh so as above so below way*,

She is blind so we cannot see her.

Portrait of The Poet as a Punchbag

I certainly dealt
With that bully,

Did you see how
I hit him in the fist
With my face?

Then I kicked his
Steel capped boot
With my ribs.

I bet his *Doc Martins*
Will hurt tomorrow.

If he'd had a knife

I would have stabbed
His blade with my body.

If he'd had a *glock*
I would have shot
His gun with
My bullet wound.

Even decapitated his axe
With my neck
If necessary.

That'll teach him
No one picks on this wimp
And gets away with it.

You Have Been Misinformed

This may seem strange to you
But the human head

Was not designed as a receptacle
For a sniper's bullet.

Yes, I know it's hard to believe
But, on the contrary,

It was actually made to hold
A sense of wonder and

An immense intellectual curiosity.
It's an easy mistake to make.

But don't take my word for it.
Look it up in a book or *Google* it.

Hard Cheese

Two women
at the
deli counter,
busy slicing
wedges of
Wensleydale
arranging
displays of
smoked
Bavarian
and apple
smoked
Cheddar.
As the wire cuts
through the
waxy flesh
of Gouda, one
of them, with
a sigh, tells
the other
about her
wayward
daughter,
she's ruined her life.
To which
her friend
replies,
Yes, but it's not
the first time
she's done it.

Don't You Have Any Mirrors In Your House?

Who is this man hanging on this cross?
Who is this woman raped by invaders?

Who are these unarmed civilians gunned
Down and thrown into a roadside ditch?

Who are these uncaring politicians?
Who are these men with
blood on their hands?

Who is this
man hanging
on a cross?

Don't you recognise me?

Don't you even recognise yourself?
Don't you have any mirrors in your house?

Strictly Sleep Dancing

He dances with her in her sleep.

Her dress is a fine mist billowing
        about her body like a rumour.

In the waking world he has two left feet
But here inside the ballroom of her head

They move through torturous tangos
            and sinuous sensual sambas.

Here he is as weightless as Astaire,
        a gravity-defying Gene Kelly.

He dances with her in her sleep but
        she never remembers her dreams.

In the morning she wonders why the
            heels and soles of her shoes
Keep wearing down at an alarming rate.

This Poem Should've Had a Better Title

Everywhere is exactly like this.
Nowhere is exactly like this.

Both of these comments are true.

There is an air-conditioned supermarket.
There is a game show on TV.

There is a burning village.
There is a soldier with a machete.

There should be a better title
                        at the top of the page.

I am beginning to repeat myself.

There is a burning village
There is a soldier with a machete

This poem had its head hacked off.

MAGINALIA

Marginalia

1.
In The Book of the Hours of the Virgin,
A bored looking nun picks penises from

A phallus tree, piling her wicker basket
Full of strange fruit as if they were

Nothing more than apples and pears.
She will labour for centuries imprisoned;

Marginalised, until the ink fades on the
Vellum, the harvest never to be consumed.

2.
A knight in full armour battles a giant snail
                    .... of course.

3.
In the margin of the Psalter, the devil holds
A sack containing all the notes that the monks

Are forbidden to sing, as if taunting them to
Elaborate.
            It's too early for baroque!

4.
In the quiet of the scriptorium
The scribe in a state of ennui,
Doodles delinquent simians,
Gatherings of gyrfalcons,
Cats with crossbows kill canine foes,
Wodwoes from the wildwood.
An owl wears a bishop's mitre
And a man vomits a shower of toads.

In the quiet of the scriptorium
The scribe's quill pours on the
Parchment Blemmyes pilfered from
The pages of Pliny and dog-headed
Men from edges of the known world.

In the quiet of the scriptorium
He imagines unheard sounds: a hare
Beats a frame drum, a goat blows a
Shofar horn, a dog plays a bagpipe,
A smiling skeleton turns the wheel on
A hurdy-gurdy's drone strings.

5.
Here a lion lies down with a lamb
While a blue monkey lifts up
The jungle king's tail to check his royal arse,

While a second monkey inserts a stick
Into the first monkey's anus.

Here a flatulent monk farts gold coins.
All this decorates the holiest of texts.

Here there are more bums out of windows
Than in all of Chaucer's pilgrims' tales.

6.
This safety valve needed loosening
Just a little, or the steam would burst the pipes.

This is the same dark trickster energy
That will pour into the Fool's Mass,

Where a child or simpleton was elected
Lord of Misrule, or a goat crowned king.

                    The Fool's Mass,
Where the congregation brayed like
Donkeys during the *Kyrie Eleison*

And played dice on the high altar
After using it as a table to eat

                    greasy street food.

When these proceedings were banned,
It moved to the *Commedia dell' Arte*
Wearing new masks and a false nose,

From there into *Guignol* shows in French parks
And Punch and Judy at the English seaside:

That's the way to do it! That's the way to do it!
That's the way to do it! That's the way to do it!

The Eighth Day

On the eighth day he woke up.
  It had just been a nightmare.

Now to do it for real!

Anticipation

She anticipated poetry
But when he touched her

It was only prose.

Cat

A midnight cat patrolling.
The moon has her single pale eye on him.

Lady, don't blink.

Picti

Pict

ure

people,
the soldiers on
The Wall called them. On a crisp
Cold night on the watchtower, a guard
Might pull his woollen cloak a little
Tighter about him to keep out the
Northern chill, dreaming of the eternal
City (that he had never seen) or perhaps
His Sarmatian homeland on the steppes,
As he kept a watchful eye on the dark;
Where there might be *Picti*, painted
In woad and tattooed, just as the tribes
Of the south had been before the
Civilising hand of the *Pax Romana,*
It's said that The Ninth once marched
North from here and vanished as if
Into mist. That guard might shiver
As he imagines their heads adorning
The lodge of some chieftain (along
With their Imperial Eagle standard)
His Sarmatian homeland suddenly
Seems further away than usual; and
Didn't his own people adorn their
Bodies with designs? Like many of
The Sixth he had *the sword in the stone*
Inked onto his forearm and rode
Behind the burnished dragon head.

Pict

   ure

      people
          bearing bright barbarous
Bling, born into battle. They'd been
Here since the white giant lay down
And green grass grew over his body;
But before the last legionnaire would
Leave to shore up his failing empire,
A new enemy would take a foothold
In the west (the *Scoti)* and absorb the
People of the looking glass and comb.
I wonder if a race could disappear so
Completely from the face of the earth
To be absorbed without a trace;
So only their name remains and even that
Appellation was given to them by Rome.
No one knows what they called themselves.
I climb a steep hill and push through
A wood so thick that no light could
Penetrate; moss spongy under my boots;
(I took a photo in that unearthly gloom
With a flash, when the film was developed
Everything came out a strange purple)
Then breaking out into a clearing
I see the stone, carved with Z-rods and
Whorls, double discs, horses and boars
As I run my fingers over the glyphs
Feeling the raised lines and deep cuts.
I like to think that something remains
Beneath the layers of Irish and Viking,
Something slight in the accent perhaps,
Below the Gaelic and the Norse.

Josephine and His Brothers

For Philip Ridley

My brothers never liked me.
I wasn't the right shape.

They said my skin was too soft.
My eyes were too big.

They complained that my thighs were
Too luminous and they had to wear
Sunglasses when looking at them.

It made them uncomfortable.

I told them they didn't need to look.

They once found a delicate and
Intricate shell on the beach
They said it was: *wonderful*.

Then they smashed it with a rock.

I saw a LGBTQ+ flag; stole it
I made a dress out of it.

My brothers sold me to an Egyptian.

It wasn't so bad. I made a good
Living interpreting dreams.

SEASONAL

1. Spring

A song leaves a
Wound in the air

A sky made of
Sleep wakes up

Crocus purple
Clouds split into
Apple-sweet yellow

As you pose
Holding a daffodil
Against your black

Polo neck sweater

2. Jasper Summer

Dumbledores bumble about
The lavender and lion's teeth,

An upturned glass upon the
Table a Jasper trapped beneath.

When I get up to leave I will
Lift his prison; let him buzz free.

I try not to harm annoying insects
Be they wasp or be they bee.

Dumbledore = Kentish for bumble bee
Jasper = Kentish for wasp
Lion's teeth = dent-de-lion
Norman French for a Dandelion

3. Autumn

Morning and more leaves fall like
Cornflakes from a sky-blue packet.

There's a spicy tang in the air and
An occasional dry flop as another drops.

Chlorophyll removes her green mask
Carotenoids and their xanthic sisters

Now have their turn to briefly shine.
Time to listen to Yves Montand's voice

Singing Prévert's lyric, but of course
Those were fallen heroes in disguise.

4. Winter

Waking into a snow-silent world where

The wind is a silver thorn piercing a red rose.

Leaving the high drift of the duvet

You put on a white coat and

                    the territory changes.

Skeletal trees acquire aquabobs.

The frozen crunch under our boots as

We walk in a realm where snow carries the

        primordial memory of water.

Aquabob = Kentish for Icicle

5. Frostrosir

There is a rose
that only blooms below zero,
When the window glass
becomes opaque,
More like the surface
of a frozen lake
Which you are looking
down upon, not out
From your little house,
where the stove is warm.
See the swirling
white bees of the
Snow Queen's swarm.

There is a rose
that only blooms below zero.
Petals that spread
on the windowpane
Icy, intricate as lace,
patterns that you trace
With a frozen finger
as you starwhisper:
Its Icelandic name,
so only the North Wind
Can hear:
Frostrosir.

6. Bottle Rockets

Jack Frost, whom I believed was a
Real person, pinched my toes.

I'd seen a picture of him and knew
He had white spiky hair and a long
                            icicle for a nose.

I'd once caught a glimpse of him
Out of the corner of my eye,
                painting the grass white.

The fifth of November, one of the few
Occasions we kids were allowed out
At night; an adventure by flashlight.

Eyes wide and round as Catherine wheels
That held the imprint of the trails
Our sparklers painted on the air.

We watched the blaze begin until all
The piled up broken fruit boxes from
The farm were eaten by the hungry flames.

Beyond the flickering circle, where
The light of the bonfire did not quite
Reach, I felt the presence of ancient
Corn ghosts from a time when it was
Not a Guy Fawkes atop the fire;

When our pagan ancestors would pass
Cattle and sheep through the smoke
Of *bone* fires, to bless the herd.

All too soon and the roman candle's rain
Of golden sparks was spent and the final
                    oohs and *aahs* were uttered.

We returned to our homes where the
Buttery electric light seemed to exorcise
The evening's magic, warding it with
            the rule of forty-watt normalcy.

On such a night there might be hot soup
Or bangers and mash, *Dixon of Dock Green*
On the black and white telly, and of course

Much later, dreams of bottle rockets that
Could reach all the way to the stars.

Next day was just as much a ritual for me
And my friends as we walked around the
Village finding scorched sticks from rockets,

Rekindling the enchantment; wondering
How far up they had travelled; from which
Far off garden they were launched.

7. Seasonal

In the supermarket aisle the
Seasons have run together
Like a Biblical prophecy.

I walk the ley line of
November between
Remaindered Halloween
Spiders and pumpkins
And the first blooms of
Tinsel and Christmas cards.

Long before the last holly
Wreath un-decks its hall
Chocolate eggs will be laid.
Hot cross buns are now
Available all year round.

I need some sunglasses
Having just had an eye
Operation but I am told
*Sorry we don't stock them
Because they are seasonal.*

Outside the sun is bright
On this clear autumn day.

MASQUE

1. Masks

I went to a fancy-dress party
Disguised as myself
But nobody recognised me.
At midnight when we removed
Our masks I took off my face.

Still nobody knew me.
This raincoat is not even mine.
I search in its pockets
For clues but instead all I find are

Gnostic fire baptisms,
Pebbles inscribed with
The names of seven powers.
Chrysanthemums,
Dog-headed snapdragons.
Spells written in baboonish.

The stairs were littered with
So many glass slippers that
I almost slipped on them
Or slipped them on
I can't remember which.

I quite often pretend to be myself.

2. Planes

The *crema* on the surface of a black coffee.
The distant borborygmus traffic that is
Always somewhere off stage; in the wings.
Rain patters on the window while simultaneously
In the unopened notebook on the table, it is a
Summer day in a different country and the only
Noise emanates from hosts of cicadas.
The two planes slide and intersect, and I am not
On either of them, as at the moment I'm standing
In an eighteen-year-old body at the centre of
A snow-covered field in the village of my youth,
Smoking a cigar and wearing too much aftershave
(both being presents given to me on Christmas day)
This younger me is imagining the future as this older
Me is imagining the past, wondering where I
Actually am, the *who*, the *what* and the *why* of me.
The three planes slide together, and I return.
Our atmosphere, I am told, is the depth
Of a breath misting the surface of a glass marble
The *crema* on the surface of a black coffee.

3. Names

Surname
Given name
Christian name
First name
Last name
Forename
Nick name
Code name
Good name
Bad name
Username
False name
Forgotten name
Holy name
Secret name
Alias
A.K.A
Nom de plume
Nom de guerre
What shape
Am I
Inside
My name?

4. Mirrors

She's as true as the north and her hair yellow as butter. While talking of masks and mirrors she remarked, *one Conceals, the other reflects*. I think she's eighty percent right but sometimes they exchange functions.

When we wear a mask, it also wears us. Some masks are worn inside the face. Mirrors, like cameras, have always lied as often as they have told the truth.

She is as true as the north and her hair yellow as butter. Unlike me, she is what she appears to be. I am always a mask.

5. Face Hat

Critics said the chimps
In the experiment
Were just *aping* the scientists.

Washo (a chimpanzee
That had been taught sign language)
Was shown a photo of a duck.

His keeper asked: *what is it?*

Washo didn't know the word,

He signed: *Water Bird.*

His keeper then held up a mask
       and asked: *what is it?*

Washo had not been taught
How to sign: *mask,*

He signed back: *A face hat.*

6. Whose Voice?

You find a poem in a book.
You read it out loud.

Whose voice do you hear?

The poet's, yes of course,
        but what other voice?

Yours, yes of course,
        that's obvious.

There is another voice;
        a third voice.

Whose voice is it?

If you know the answer
Then you are probably a poet.

You have to figure it out yourself.

I am not going to tell you.

Here

Not so much a pipe dream but
Perhaps perceived in the smoke
Of Hilary Halpern's
                    Havana cigar:

A house of inspiration beneath
            the synagogue of stars.

Under its roof artists mix
            like pigments on a pallet.

Here coffee-fuelled discussions
Give birth to countless creations;

Food makes memories;
Literature breeds empathy
            and visual art delights the eye.

Here is the nucleus of our
            collective creativity.

*Commissioned by The Halpern Trust to commemorate the
20th Anniversary of the founding of Nucleus Arts*

In The Voices of the Estuary

for Philip Kane

Here every guitar has a Medway twang.
There are found poems in the corner shop.

On the salt marsh a drunken Siren sang.
Even our glottal stop has a glottal stop.

In these voices of the estuary their
Was is where their *were* should be.

Even the half-submerged *Asda* shopping cart
Finds its way into a certain poet's art.

The river's so wide you think you're by the sea
And it's also in the voices of the estuary.

La Matadora

You followed that woman
Who dressed in armour.

On her flag, a *fleur-de-lis.*

I am a bull to her La Matadora,
Sometimes the matador is me.

Zeus carries off poor Europa,
The Olympian's mind was on rape.

I am a bull to her La Matadora,
There's a sword concealed in her cape.

You ask me, who is speaking?
Whose voice do I hear today?

I am a bull to her La Matadora
I fall as the crowd cries *Olé.*

Delia

for Delia Derbyshire 1937-2001

Psyche-Delia I can
Now put a face to

Time-And-Relative
Dimensions-In-Space.

You radio-phonic
And ultra-sonic
Sorceress of sound,

I heard your siren song
My bags are packed
And I am Skaro bound.

Mint Tea and *Kief*

The blind man in the marketplace wears
Dark glasses and a fez; he sings and
Accompanies his voice with a fiddle.
He only knows one song. It's about a
Lost or possibly a stolen passport.
Some people just pay him to go away.

A storyteller tells a tale of Sinbad with
Puppets but later swaps to *Star Wars*,
Using action figures as props. As Pablo said:
Good artists borrow but great artists steal.

William was an American writer.
He was so thin that if you looked at him
Sideways he was invisible. He invented
The terms *heavy metal* and *blade-runner*
And once shot his wife in the head
While pretending to be William Tell.
At night he smokes *kief* and his typewriter
Morphs into a creature like a giant cockroach.

Mint tea is like drinking a *polo* mint.
Houses painted blue can give you some
Protections from *djinn;* or else you can wear
The Hand of Fatima around your neck.
I've tasted mint tea but not smoked *kief*.
I've never been to Morocco
                    but I still wrote this.

The Blue Hand Upon the Yellow Box of Sound

In memory of Chris Broderick

From now on, others will sing your songs.
Only we who knew you
        will hear your voice under theirs.

Punk-folk ballads that could be as savage
As a claw-hammer prising open a crate
Or as tender as the low November sun
Giving a gift of unexpected warmth.
        Signs of a complex nature at work.

We remember the blue hand upon
        the yellow box of sound.
By the catalpa tree on the stage,
With several hundred people singing along
About girls who comb their hair
        With a raven's wing.

Medway delta dreams and lyrics that taste
Of salt and seaweed;
        Fairgrounds and Ferris wheels,
And always running through them,
As it runs through our region;
        Our towns: that river that names us.

To quote that song you wrote for your
Father: *So long, me old china.*

Afterwards

Will you rend your clothes and put ash on your sleeve?

Will you climb down the inverted ziggurat into the
Earth where I hang on a peg in my sister's kitchen?

Will you cover all the mirrors in creation and make the
        plants swear a solemn oath
                                (even the mistletoe)?

Will you forgive me for ingesting a few measly
                                pomegranate seeds?

Will you look back before we reach the surface?

Will you read all the books to me that were published
After I left for the land of silence,
                not knowing if I can even hear you?

Will café owners tell their customers: *that's his chair,*
        that's where he wrote his incomprehensible garbage?

    and he still owes me for seven black coffees!

The Recurring Dream of The
Knife Thrower's Assistant

The radio plays *Thirteen Mexican Angels in*
The Valley of the Sun and she is not wearing
A blindfold. Her face feels naked, not nude.

She's strapped to the spinning target, but it's
His wife and not him whose hands blossom
With a bouquet of throwing knives and looking
At her with jealous eyes. *Like daggers*, she thinks.

She feels like wet silk that had been pulled
Too taut and might rip at any moment.
As she spins, the sequins on her limbs sparkle
The ruby in her navel feels like a bullseye.

She wakes in her caravan and gets dressed in a
Hurry, packing her bag and departs without leaving
A goodbye note. In her next job she will be an
Aerialist or be fired from a cannon. Something safe.

But I Do Believe in Ghosts, She Said

I stand somewhere between the clockwork man
                              and the bright burning tiger.

                         The newly minted sun shines in the
Cobalt blue purse of the sky
                              like out-of-reach legal tender.

I am eating olives from a brown paper bag as I
                              stroll around a Spanish market
when she tells me that she does *not*
                              believe in the immortal soul.

She says: *when you are dead you are just dust.*
                              Nothing remains, but
She adds *I do believe in ghosts.*

When these words are on her lips she looks like
        The Mother of Owls in the darkest part of noon.

I stand between the candle and the star. I find myself
wondering if it is time to sweep up the shadows from
beneath the trees and put them in a box file.

A Stranger in Paradise

"I have come to douse the fires of hell
And burn away the promise of paradise"
                    —*Rabia Al Basri*

I don't believe in heaven as a place
But if it were true I would have to
Enter as an illegal immigrant, with
No documentation and a forged passport.

After all I have already married an Angel
So I should be eligible for *Green Card.*

            On the test for citizenship
I'd need to pretend that white is my
Favourite colour, while I plot to paint
The Celestial city red instead,
Biting my tongue as I listen to sermons
            by sanctimonious saints.

But if you were there, as you surely
Would be, I would grit my teeth and
Go with the flow while secretly reading
Banned books at night by flashlight.

The Scent of Meaning

The word *is* comes from
The Sanskrit root *as*
Meaning to breathe,

That is: *to exist.*

Not comes from the word *na*
Meaning: *to perish.*

The bottle is empty
But the scent lingers.

When a modern English
Person says: *that's weird*
They mean it is strange and
Beyond explaining.

When a heathen Anglo-Saxon
Said: that is *wyrd*
They meant it is strange
But the right person
       could read it.

The bottle is empty
But the scent lingers.

Reality Check

The sparrows do not have
                          Twitter accounts
      or hedge fund managers.

The bull and the bear do not care if
                     the stock market is up
           or down.

The trees do not read the *Financial Times*.

The badger and the fox spend zero hours
               on their mobile phones
      and *Facebook.*

The middle class may live
                     in gated communities
      but so do cattle and sheep.

The Sun Boat

It moved across the sky
From orient to occident.

The boat was powered by
Many chimpanzees typing

On Remington typewriters.
A by-product of this was the

Occasional complete set
Of Shakespeare's plays

But they were easily tossed
Over the side and fell to earth.

In The Surrealist's Garden

In the surrealist's garden the sparrows plot
To catch a cat and eat it.

Ghosts are pegged on the washing line
Until they are dry.

Foxes lounge around reading French paperbacks,
Bees hum songs by Georges Brassens.

In the Surrealist's garden nothing
Unusual ever happens and even poets get bored.

Your Name Feels Strange in My Mouth

I don't want your name in my mouth,

It does not taste of the same colour anymore.

I don't want you tripping off the tip of my tongue.

I want to forget how to pronounce you correctly.

I don't want your name in my mouth.
Your consonants are too hard on me.

Your long vowels too elastic to chew upon.

I don't want your name in my mouth.
I spit you out.

But there is still a bitter aftertaste.

free wings with every order

free wings with every order/ on my third
glass of *pike creek* it sounded like a good deal/

with them i might fly up into the starrymost
heights of the high & dusty summer where the
daughters of the bearded dream pour out
water from the jars of heaven/on
the night of nights/
when all the portals of paradise are open
& the rain is sweet upon the tongue/

i 'd look down the back of some celestial
settee & find my lost silver & turquoise ring/
that i have shed so many tears
over/over the years/
i don't tell any of this to the waitress/
the ice clinked in my drink as i sipped my
bourbon /aged in barrels that had once
contained rum/ or so the label claims/
& i try to catch the waitress's eye/

free wings with every order/ it sounded
like a good deal but the menu lied.

Fragments of Nocturnal Conversations

1.

—I haven't seen you for such a long time
—That's because I'm dead

—Then how are you here?
—It's a dream, silly.

—Oh, I see. Shall I put the kettle on?
—Ooh a nice cup of tea and a biscuit.

2.

—That white lace dress I saw in Canterbury.
—What about it?
—It haunted me.

3.

—I dreamed about spiders all night.
—So?
—In the morning I found a leg in my moustache.

Ends And Beginnings

The water that just slid down my throat,
Carrying my daily regime of pills,

Once also slid down a dinosaur's back
As rain on some un-named day
In the Jurassic period.

Some Kabbalists believed in
A garden called *Eden* at the beginning,
And one called *Pardes* at the end.

All that separates them is merely time.

I often wonder if I am at the end
And this life is just me remembering.

My definition of Hell is calling out
Your name in the dark and not
Hearing your voice answer.

A Tale of Two Muses

She loved this conjuror of Christmas ghosts
She was the woman from the *Frozen Deep.*

I think she haunts his prose
             in almost as many assumed names
     as she had to wear in life.
Covers for their clandestine love (a fate
       she shared with Chatham and Rochester).

In print she was Estella, Bella, Lucie and
           In that last mystery: Helena Landless,

A play on words, perhaps, referencing her
         father's middle name of Lawless?

She was even there at the railway crash
That pulled *The Signalman* from his pen.

He returned to the place of his *childhood fancy,*
The magic taproot of his art: the Medway Towns
                 was his first muse
  But Ellen was the second;
        one explicit the other implicit.

He was immortalised in merchandise,
All those *ivorex* plaques:
      She only exists behind the mask of fiction.

Commissioned by Wordsmithery for The Medway Council as part of the Dickens 150th Anniversary Empty Chair Project.

Despatches From a Place of Rainbows and Shadows

1.
Sephie said, *that's my bag,*
Why is the shadow holding my bag?

Her mum: *try explaining*
To a two-and-a-half-year-old
That her shadow had not
            stolen her bag.

2.
Sephie just said out of the blue,
If we run out of food, we'll have
To eat people and astronauts and
                spiky hedgehogs.

3.
Joe's youngest, looking around our
front room said:
    your house is a place of
                rainbows and shadows.

4.
Lianna likes her *half-a-monkey-car,*
But she has yet to get a tune out of it.

5.
Siena's letter: *Dear Santa,*
Please can I have a real live unicorn,
And could you please
          bring my cat back to life?
If not I will like anything you give me.
   You probably know what's best.

6.
Siena tells me that she will be a vet
When she grows up,
But only for mythological animals
Like mermaids and gryphons

7.
Edith woke from
A bad dream and said,
The worms are crying for the world.
Then she went straight back to sleep.

8.
Overheard on a train,
In between giggles, a little girl exclaims:
Please don't eat her, she's my friend.

9.
From this place of thunderstorms,
Spiders, gingerbread houses and tears,
Shimmering stars and splashing
In puddles on rainy days,

You can see the roots of poetry.

Mr Cloud and Mr Leopard

Hey Mr Cloud
Why can't you see?

My vision is
Cloudy obviously.

Hey Mr Leopard
Where are you at?

I ignored the
King James Bible

I changed my spots

Now I'm just
Another cat.

MARIANNE

Marianne

I'll take the train to nineteen sixty-eight to see
                                                        if you're still there,
Standing at the barricade with your Juliet Greco
Hair tied back in a chignon, the colour of night.
You looked so good in black and white, as the riot
Squad approach, ready for the fight. An image
That comes to me, triggered by the scent of coffee
Or tobacco or fresh baked bread, in a time now
So cynical when that romantic cause is dead.

Serge

There is a hole in France
Shaped like you,
That no one can fill

Still, after all this time,
You are everywhere, *broken*
Into a thousand pieces of voice.

Serge, only you could find
A rhyme for *Kleenex*
In the French language.

Serge, they just announced
That they are making *Metro*
Tickets digital, but at least

We still have cabbages.

Brel

Outside the little museum
Dedicated to him, there is
A life-size statue of Jacques
In a pose of performance,
On stage with a microphone,
At his feet a record player;
A woman's shoe, thrown
On stage by a fan, all cast
In bronze; weathered green
By the elements and time.
On this afternoon beneath
A damp grey sky, flat as the
Flanders land in Brel's song
Marieke, a young couple with
A teenage daughter stand by
The sculpture; all three
In an attitude of reverence.
The mother holds up her
I-Phone; presses play and
Ne Me Quitte Pas flows from
                    her iTunes app.
I watch her face with its
Expression of rapture. It is
The look of a woman in love
With someone who died
Decades before she was born.
I think there is something
Almost like religion here.
We stand, the five of us, the family,
I and my wife Ann in the drizzle
As Jacques Brel's voice begs
His lover *not to leave him now*.

La Llorona

Where are your children Llorona?
I left them at the river.

Where are your children Llorona?
Border Control took them.

Where are your children Llorona?
The president put them in cages.

Where are your children Llorona?
They are running from the Cartels.

Where are your children Llorona?
They are living la loca vida.

Where are your children Llorona?
A Coyote holds their debt.

Where are your children Llorona?
They are sun-sweat and moon-tears
They were the past and they are the future.

Imanni Da Silva

Imanni, her lilac dress seemingly ablaze
From the fierce eye of the Angolan sun,

Her shades perched upon her head.
On the table inches away from those
Long, elegant, manicured fingers,
A cold glass sweats beads of ice.

Imanni on the runway
                    in super model mode,
Or as an artist, a writer, an activist,
A Renaissance woman in more than one way
Having been born twice (once from a
        womb, the other by a surgeon's skill)
Her cousin Maria told me that *no one ever*
Thought of her as male; even when
    she was a child she was like a little girl.

Imanni walked into the exhibition in
London where my paintings hung and
Every man and several women turned
To gaze at her in a way I wished they had
Looked at my art.
              A silent **WOW** hung in the air.

Imanni Da Silva the machete against the
Gear as the yellow star of plenty burns
On the red and black flag,

Imanni is a guitar made blue by dusk in a
Citrus grove, where on the trees ripe oranges
        burn like miniature suns.

Coyote's Last Poem

For Sherman Alexie

No more *Acme* catalogue!
I got that damn bird at last.
He's roadkill, he's lunch.

No more fucking fake
       Dream Catchers
Made in Taiwan and sold to
Betty and Veronica who are
Really, really into ethnic.

My last purchase from *Acme*
Was a *Build Your Own*
           Time Machine Kit
I went back and
Sank the *Santa Maria*
I sank the *Pinta*
       and the *Niña* too
Goodbye Columbus
No more *Lucky Strikes*
No more Madison admen.
No more public relations.
No more Lone Ranger.
No more John Wayne.
No more wagon trains.
No more iron horse.
No more *yippee ki yay!*
No more Manhattan Project.
Now I'm learning how
       to draw Tex Avery,
Let's see how he likes it.

Memory Biscuit

Every day out on the walk
The dog stops at the same place.

His owner says: *two years ago*
Someone gave him a biscuit here.

Note To Self

Old fool of a poet
Stop counting syllables.

Crack open the haiku.

Cold Tea

The tea in my cup is cold.
The hours ran away.

Where did the day go?

KINO

i. ode to the technicolor camera

Thou box of rainbows,
Your heart is a prism

Splitting light and reflecting
Twenty five percent
Onto the green record,

The other seventy five
Onto the red and the blue.

Jack painted Ava's lips
Scarlet and used

The moon for her key light.

He breathed on your lens
And called up a fog

For dragon ships to hide in.

Thou box of rainbows

In the magic hour
Jack learned all your mysteries.

ii. noir

1.

These two men walking toward the rooming house
Could be Gestapo or Secret Police from some
Iron curtain country or maybe just hired killers.

Beyond the fourth wall many of the technicians,
Who light these swirls of cigarette smoke and
Casablanca fog, making them magical in monochrome,
Are themselves refugees from nightmare States.

And these actors sweating under the arc lights
May have also performed in a real theatre of war.
Does the camera pick up any of this
                          in their micro-expressions?

Last night I dreamed I went back in time to
Assassinate Hitler; I waited in a dark alley
With my Saturday night special
                          (Its serial number filed off)
But the *Führer* never appeared in that scene.
He must have been edited out in a rewrite.

2.
On the set Sinatra keeps needling
Broderick Crawford about

His weight until he can't
Take it any longer and snaps, pinning

Frank to the floor, he rips off the
Crooner's toupee with his teeth

And in his rage begins to chew
It until he starts to choke on

The hairpiece, eventually
Coughing it up like a cat with a furball.

3.
Fred can't take his eyes off of
                    Barbara's ankle chain
            and because of it,
                        neither can we.

4.
Venetian blinds tiger stripe office walls
Vivisecting my body with razor sharp shadows.

Eros and Thanatos are handcuffed to each other.

Oh take me across the kitchen table
While I listen for the postman's ring.

Lee Marvin's gun has a phallic silencer.

I tried to use my charms but he said:
     Lady I don't have the time.

    He's *Death* and I am *The Maiden.*

But to be fair I did try to have him
     murdered in the previous scene.

waked.   *greased.*   *fixed.*

   rubbed-out.   *wasted.*

5.
Montage shot of neon reflections on wet sidewalks:

El Morocco.   **Blue Parrot.**   **Copacabana.**

Zanzibar.   **Shamrock.**

White raincoats lacquered by rain, mixed with milk
to make it visible to the lens.

(*after dancing in that deluge*
            Gene Kelly's suit must have smelled sour.)

Light from some unknown source casts the shadows
Of intricate ironwork that may (or may not exist.)

The ghost of Dr Caligari has come to the talkies.

6.
In *Woman On The Run* (1947)

Description?
                asks the Detective.

He wore a snap brimmed hat
                and a suit, she replies

The cop gives a look that seems to say,

In 1947 almost every man does.

7.
On a *Violent Saturday*

                  he took a walk to

Where The Sidewalk Ends.

It was an

             Experiment Perilous.

He had a *Glass Key* to unlock a

                  Lady in The Lake.

She was *Ice Blonde* in a

               Crimson Kimono

A short walk to a

               Pickup on South Street.

iii. giallo

In *The House of Laughing Windows,*
       by *The Mill of the Stone Women*

In *The Short Night of the Glass Dolls,*

The Eye in the Labyrinth opens
       like a *Flower with Steel Petals*

To let in *All the Colours of the Dark.*

You bring me
       Five Dolls for an August Moon

   and *Seven Orchids of Blood.*

Your flesh is touched by *The Iguana*
       with a Tongue of Fire.

You are my *Bird with the Crystal Plumage.*

I am a *Butterfly with Blood-Stained Wings.*

iv. technicolor

      The red-haired ventriloquist is leaving on
the midnight plane to Zurich
The plans are glued into Clarence's head
(Or are they in Terrence's head?)
This is bound to cause a confusion
              of Shakespearean proportions.
The fog at the airport has a bluish tinge
Due to the limitations of 1950's Technicolor

      The red-haired ventriloquist is accosted
By the spy who introduces himself: *Gromik,*
He answers him: *gesundheit.*
The audience laughs. I look around but all
The worn velveteen seats are empty.
I am alone in the cinema.
The Ritz was pulled down years ago to
Make way for a bus station but for tonight
It has been reconstructed just for me.

      The red-haired ventriloquist is now
On the run from foreign agents
             and an evil psychiatrist.
I want to tell you how much I love this movie
But then I remember I haven't met you yet.
When the feature ends, I walk out into
The foyer with its gold-painted plaster-framed
Photos of the stars and the counter where,
Earlier, I bought a tub of vanilla ice cream.

When I leave the building the picture palace
Deconstructs and the bus station rebuilds itself
Like a piece of time lapse film.
I must wait many years to discuss the movie
With you. I walk through *La Nuit Americaine*
Under a sky made twilight by a filter on
The lens where fat white clouds glow like
        radioactive sheep in a cobalt blue field.

Jianghu

1.
Rivers and lakes in an alternative existence
Where the law of gravity is not enforced;

Where every gangster is affiliated with triads
And secret societies with roots in feudal times.

Violent ballets of bullets and steel stars
Unfold in slow motion and widescreen.

In the secret cinema of unknown pleasures,
Housed in the house of flying daggers.
I let the electric dreams into my eyes.

2.
Oh, Madam Cheng, your slit to the hip *cheongsam*
Is so very tight on your boyish body.
When I told you that there was an American
Comic book character called *The Dragon Lady*
You laughed and said, *all dragons are male,*
Including the one on your dress which seems
To shimmer and caress you when you move.

Oh, Madam Cheng you are every inch a woman
Except for the three you keep concealed.
I dreamed that embroidered dragon moved
Over your ivory nakedness like a living tattoo.

Oh, Madam Cheng you sip your *oolong** tea
And say: *now yang flows through my yin.*

**oolong* means black dragon.

Mermaid

She was the kind of woman
Whom old men, who wear
Strange hats and sport beards,
Might paint on bits of driftwood.

You might meet her amongst
The sand dunes in a run down
Coastal resort in the winter.

You might share a *Senior Service* or
A flask of strong tea with her
As you lament the passing
            of the town's derelict pier,

While the blue hands of the wind draw
Curtains of rain across a sky that
Wears a necklace of gull cries.

In the amusement arcade
Jolly Jack Tar laughs maniacally
                in his glass case.
Waves pound against
        the rotten Victorian breakers.

You might try not to look at her legs
Between her boots and the hem
Of her mackintosh but it is obvious
She does not have the tail of a fish,

And yet there is something of the
Sea about her as she speaks
Of starfish in the sky-deep ocean;
    those dark depths where the mind
Of the octopus dwells on things
No human can fathom.

She sings of combs and looking glasses
Of drowned sailors and you imagine
Cold water closing around your head.

Church Street

Light is the mother of the eye
And the father of darkness.

Death is annoyed with me
Because I never learned to play chess.

Here there is more river and more sky.

I am old in a new house,
Hemmed by green parks
On a hill sloping towards the Medway.

I once sipped the black milk
Of midnight and tincture of owl.

I once walked ghost roads asking strangers:
How many miles to Babylon?

I once walked *three score and ten*
By candlelight and earthlight
                    there and back again.

Now I drink coffee and watch TV

I avoid going out at night, but if I must
I carry a flashlight instead of a candle.

These days I limp on streets that
                    are made ordinary by failure.

An old man wrote this poem.

Ann's View

A single sailboat seen white
Against the slate grey water;

Wildfowl and wading birds
   wintering in the wetlands.

A breeze blows the reeds
At the edge of the salt marsh.

Closer to our shore, Shelducks
With their Sheldrakes, Dunlin,

Oystercatchers and Avocets
Search for food in the silt at low tide.

The river wears a different dress
Every day; never quite the same
Hue of blue, green, silver or grey.

   The distant fort, sometimes
Seeming closer; sometimes further.
Ready for an invasion that never came.

The view belongs to Ann
But she allows me to look at it.

Look For Me Yesterday

Look for me yesterday,
That is where I will be.

In the garden of a café
That is no longer there
At a table beneath a tree,
With a book open and
My coffee getting cold.
Look for me yesterday
When none of us were old.

Don't go to tomorrow
You will not see my face.
Don't go to tomorrow
You will not find a trace.
Don't go to tomorrow
Where my work's no longer read.
Go where great poets live,
Go to yesterday instead.

Photo by Ann Lewis

Author's Note

Almost all of the poems in this book were written since the publication of *The Long Ago and Eternal Now* in 2017. I say almost because there are two stowaways in this collection. In 2019 Colony Press launched volume one of my collected poems 1975 - 2005 which, with my previous two collections, should have meant all my poetry to date was in print. Should have; however recently while looking through some of the anthologies my work has appeared in, I found one poem that I had completely forgotten about.

The poem titled *Hedge* was published in *The Best Horror and Fantasy-Thirteenth Annual Collection* edited by Ellen Datlow and Terri Windling (St. Martins Griffin, New York) It was a big deal for me to be in a collection with authors such as Neil Gaiman, Ursula K. Le Guin and Charles De Lint and I can't imagine how I could have forgotten about this poem. It appears in this collection in a revised form. Revised because having forgotten it I had reused a line in another poem and that needed to be dealt with before it could see the light of day again.

The second stowaway is the poem *Hard Cheese*. It is one of my poems that came out of overheard conversations most of these pieces can be found in *This Love Like A Rage Without Anger*. Somehow this little poem slipped through the net but now it is found again.

In this book are three commissioned poems. The first of these is *Here* on page 85, commissioned to celebrate the 20th Anniversary of *Nucleus Arts*. Thanks to Genevieve Tullberg, David Stokes and also Aaron Telford of *Café Nucleus* for thinking of me for the job.

The second is a *A Tale Of Two Muses* on page 103 commissioned by Wordsmithery for the Medway Council as one of the 10 Dickens 150th Anniversary Empty Chair Poetry Trail pieces.

Lastly (but not least) *Poem for Simon Mills* on page 6 written for my dear friend Simon Mills, painter and printmaker and fellow member of Colony. It was commissioned by my equally dear friend the Collage artist, poet and member of Colony, Bronach Rae.

This collection also contains two poems that were translated into Italian by Silvia Pio and published in her online magazine *Margutte*.

All the artwork is by me, unless stated otherwise.

Finally, thanks to Rachel at Choir Press for her advice and patience and a huge thanks to Ann for her help and support.

Bill Lewis 2022

Biographical Notes

Bill Lewis was one of the legendary Medway Poets Group along with Billy Childish, Sexton Ming, Charles Thomson and Rob Earl.

He has performed his poems in Europe, Latin America and North America and has been published in magazines, journals and anthologies all over the world. Some of his poems have been translated into French, Spanish, Italian and his short stories into German. Silvia Pio translated his poems into Italian and they have been published in the online Magazine Margutte. In December 2020 she also published three more of Bill's poems in 'The Tree Project'.

In addition, Lewis has been broadcast on television and radio on both sides of the Atlantic, including on the guerrilla Radio Faribundo Marti in El Salvador. He has carried out readings, workshops and lectures at Literary Festivals (including the International Cambridge Poetry Festival), hospitals, prisons, schools (including the Kent Children's' University where he taught a course on mythology) and universities. Lewis was guest lecturer in Myth and Culture for The Association of Religion in Intellectual Life (ARIL) at the University of Rhode Island and also for the Social Anthropology Club at the University of Eastern Connecticut. He has recently delivered a presentation at the Kent Arts Convention.

Lewis was the first Writer-in-Residence at the Brighton Festival (1985) and was presented with the Literature Award at the Culture and Design Awards 2012.

Bill Lewis is also a visual artist and was one of the original 13 founder members of the Stuckist Movement.

He has since gone on to disseminate the ideas and theories that have emerged from Remodernism.

He has exhibited his paintings in various galleries in Paris, London, Berlin, New Jersey, Los Angeles, Kentucky and was featured in the 'Punk Victorian' exhibition at the Walker Gallery, Liverpool.

In 2017 Lewis become a member of COLONY: A Community of Artists.

www.billlewis-art.co.uk
www.colony-arts.co.uk

Other books by Bill Lewis

In The House of Ladders:
ISBN: 978-0-9571829-0-5

The Long Ago and Eternal Now:
ISBN: 978-0-9571829-2-9

This Love Like a Rage Without Anger:
ISBN: 978-1-9996948-0-7

Lightning Source UK Ltd.
Milton Keynes UK
UKHW011031161222
414000UK00003B/81